The Sun Will Rise Tomorrow

A Child's View of the Holocaust

Irit Dror-Reytan

The Sun Will Rise Tomorrow

A Child's View of the Holocaust

Irit Dror-Reytan

Irit Dror-Reytan

The Sun Will Rise Tomorrow

Dekel Publishing House
www.dekelpublishing.com

North American rights by
Samuel Wachtman's Sons, Inc.

English editing: Kathleen Roman
Graphic design: Giulio Venturi
Photographies: Avi Reytan
Proof reading: Pnina Ophir, Dory Morik

For information contact:

Dekel Publishing House
P.O. Box 6430, Tel Aviv
6106301, ISRAEL
Tel: +972 3506-3235
Fax: +972 3604-4627
Email: info@dekelpublishing.com

Samuel Wachtman's Sons, Inc.
2460 Garden Road, Suite C
Monterey, CA 93940, U.S.A.
Tel: 831 649-0669
Fax: 831 649-8007
Email: samuelwachtman@gmail.com

Table of Content

Dedication

I dedicate Renie's story to my children and grandchildren.

Why didn't I ever tell them about Renie? Maybe I was afraid—thinking they wouldn't be interested. How could I reveal the shame, the humiliation, the heartache, the trampled honor to those who could not, would not, understand?

How do you share your innermost feelings and still keep yourself whole?

Could I forgive myself for revealing Renie's darkest secrets?

First, Renie had to forgive herself, to learn, to allow herself to partake of life, not to fear retribution—to dare.

In the year 2000, I was back in school at Lesley University, in Boston in the United States, studying women's studies. "Forgiveness" was the subject of one class, and that is when it hit me. I wrote this letter to Renie:

> *My little one,*
>
> *I want to make you a promise. You will never have to fear going out again, nor be afraid to be seen. You may ask any question and not fear the answer. You may touch anyone or anything without fear of retribution. You are free to choose any way you want to go; you are free to make mistakes without fearing the consequences.*

This I give to you as a present, with my blessing—your freedom from me.

To all those abused children in the world, wherever you might be, "Don't give up. Hold onto hope—for the sun will rise tomorrow."

Irit

Last, but certainly not least, my wholehearted thanks to Avi, my husband and best friend, without whose love and support these pages would never have been written.

Irit Dror-Reytan

Sempteber 2017

Prologue

Once there was a little girl who was born into the pandemonium of WW2, in a small town in Galicia, Poland. She came into the world under a black cloud of terror, after Nazi Germany had overrun Poland and was in complete control.

Renie, for this was the name she had been given, lived for the first years of her life with her parents in a country cottage overlooking her grandmother's fields and orchards. She was loved; she was happy.

Then, in the summer of her third year, the German army marched into her home town.

Renie remembered some of the hiding places where she hid with her mother, but each time they were found by the Germans and sent to the ghetto.

Once, when she was hiding in an attic, she awoke to a shaft of sunlight slashing through the cracks in the wooden attic walls. The scene was probably as glorious as Gustav Doré's paintings—but to her the cracks enhanced her fear of being seen, uncovered, and taken away.

On beautiful summer afternoons she could hear children laugh and play—she could see through the cracks—but she had been warned never to go too near the cracks for fear of discovery.

Renie was moved from one hiding place to another, until her parents left her on a farm with the family that lived there, promising to return as soon as they could. At first her father would visit her often and bring her "goodies," but these visits became shorter and further apart, until they stopped altogether.

Renie was left all alone, with a strange family, hiding from the world.

This is her story.

Chapter 1
Renie

Road leading to Nana's & Renie's homes

Most literature claims that children seldom remember events from very early childhood. Renie, however, has very vivid pictures wrought in her memory. Every once in a while, when she is in a certain mood, they cross the panorama of her life.

One of the earliest memories is a picture of her sitting on her father's chest, which was in a plaster cast, and having her long blonde locks gently combed and caressed by his loving hands.

Renie's father had developed tuberculosis of the spine and had been in a plaster cast from his neck to his legs; he had been confined to his bed for a very long time. In fact, those were Renie's earliest memories of him, lying on his back, in his cast, brushing her hair and telling her stories.

Renie had been barely three.

Renie was an only child. She was born on September 22, 1939, during the month German troops marched into Poland. There was total confusion. She had been delivered, on the kitchen table, by the family physician.

The first years of her life were spent in their country cottage in the suburb of Boryslav (Tustanovice), a small town near Lvov. It was a pastoral area with a river running through the village, bordered on both sides by very tall weeping willows. The family had a nice garden with plum, apple, and cherry trees, and a couple of very old walnut trees. In the vegetable garden, tomatoes and other vegetables grew. Close to the cottage bedroom there was a wall of very high beanstalks from which the pods hung heavily on the vines.

Renie's Nana, her beloved grandmother, lived in the adjacent cottage. It also had a luxurious garden filled with trees, flowers, and all kinds of vegetables. Nana had a wonderful home. It had many rooms—some were called bedrooms, maybe because each one had a very big bed in it that was sooo soft—and it also had a smell that Renie loved.

Her aunts and uncles would come, with her cousins, for the holidays and they would all be together and have great fun. There was a very big kitchen in which the cooks were busy preparing special food for the holidays. Nana and the adults would sit in the living room, drinking wine, and the children would play in the rest of the house. They played hide-and-go-seek upstairs, in all the bedrooms.

Sometimes, when they were thirsty, they would tiptoe to the kitchen and ask for a drink. The housekeeper would give them each a little piece of chocolate with the drink and secretly wink at Renie, so no one would notice.

Sometimes, when the children were too noisy, someone would tell them to be more quiet, but Nana always said, "Let them have their fun, this is their time and my pleasure."

After the long meal, the children were more than ready for bed, and with help from Nanny, they were soon sound asleep.

In the morning, they were the first to wake up. The cook made sure they had a quiet breakfast, and then they went to play in the garden. They were happy. Renie spent many happy days at Nana's.

Now there were no more holidays, no visits, just Nana and Renie's parents. Renie still spent a lot of time at Nana's, but things were different.

Road leading to Nana's & Renie's homes

What puzzled Renie was that, every once in a while, Nana would hold her too tightly for comfort, as if she wanted to absorb her into her soft, warm body, whose gentle odor Renie loved.

When Renie would look into Nana's eyes, Nana would smile sadly at her. It seemed that those beautiful, kind, azure eyes would shed tears in a moment.

Nana would take her back home and sit by her father's bed and they would whisper to each other. Not that Renie cared, but it seemed odd to her—why didn't they talk as usual? Why weren't they joking, laughing? After all, Renie's father had been in bed for so long, surely he must have enjoyed the visits?

Chapter 2

The Beans Grew High That Summer

Nana's home

One morning, Renie's mother woke her, dressed her quickly, and took her to Nana's. The two women exchanged a few words and Nana immediately took Renie in her arms, briskly went into a room where she opened the floor, descended into a small, dark room, and sat down on a bench, clutching Renie to her bosom. She then, very quietly, hummed a song that was so familiar to Renie, yet through it all Renie could hear Nana's heart beat strong and fast.

They were soon joined by Renie's mother. All three sat in a tense silence.

Outside the room, there was a lot of commotion: men's voices were shouting strange words, motorcycles were *tak-tak-tak*ing, there were angry footsteps above, doors slammed—and then the motorcycles left.

There was utter silence.

After a while, the two women, with the baby, climbed out of the room under the floor and ran to Renie's cottage. They called frantically for Renie's father, searching through the house, but no one was there. The two women sat in quiet despair.

It was then that they heard his feeble voice coming from beneath the bedroom window.

A couple of neighbors came in and helped carry her father indoors. They were so relieved and happy.

Later, as they sat sipping a cup of hot tea, Renie heard Nana whisper: "Thank God the beans grew high this summer."

Chapter 3

The Change

Renie's home

Things were not the same.

Renie's relatives seldom came to visit, and when they did come, it was always after dark. The house was not lit as usual—it was dark. There were no meals in the big dining room. They all sat at the big kitchen table drinking sweet tea and eating sandwiches. There was no laughter, no jokes—everyone was serious and spoke in low voices as if trying not to awake anyone upstairs.

The adults had a lot of things to discuss and would send all the children upstairs, but they were not allowed to play their usual games and were not allowed to make any noise.

There was no cook, no gardener; only the housekeeper stayed to help Nana. They had all left.

Nana did not make her fruit preserves they so loved.

The visits became more and more rare, and then, Nana left her house.

No one picked the fruit—it was lying under the trees giving off a sweet, sickening smell.

Then Renie became ill. Her father, who was now well, took care of her. She couldn't eat, so he gave her warm goat's milk to drink.

Chapter 4
Dr. Harmelin, the "Angel of Mercy"

Renie was very ill. She had a very high temperature, she could not eat, and she found it harder and harder to breathe. All she wanted was to be left alone and to sleep. When her parents woke her so she could take her medicine, she looked at them and recognized a fear, a look of helplessness in their eyes. They changed the wet towels on her forehead, caressed her gently, and smiled bravely, with their lips, but their eyes did not smile.

Then, in the middle of the night, Renie was rudely awakened by the family doctor, Dr. Harmelin. She knew him well. He had always been so kind to her, so gentle. Now, in the middle of the night, he hurt her. He stuck a needle in her. It hurt so much! Why was he being so mean to her? Dr. Harmelin repeated those nightly visits for a whole week.

Renie hated the needle, and she allowed herself to cry. It just hurt too much—she did not want to be a brave little girl any longer. It took a long time before she was able to get up again. Renie felt better.

She slept less and drank a little broth. Mama called it the miracle medicine. It came from nature—the chicken had given up its life to save Renie's. Time was kind to Renie. She recovered from the "terrible illness" but remained weak and her pesky cough would not go away.

She spent a lot of time playing by herself in Nana's garden, in the sunshine, but when she asked where Nana was, why her door was locked, she was told that Nana had gone to Auntie Genia's for a while, that she would be back soon.

Days passed and Nana did not come back.

Renie often asked Mama why Auntie Genia and Yochi didn't come to visit. They had always come before, and Renie liked to play with Yochi. They were good friends. Yochi was her "bestest" cousin and he played the violin too!

Renie did not get an answer. Lately, she had not seen any of her uncles, aunts, or cousins. Even her beloved Nana had not come back. Where had they all gone?

Everything was so quiet. The only people she sometimes saw were their Ukrainian neighbors, whose language she understood. Although she spoke German and Polish, she did not speak Ukrainian, but even they spoke quietly and did not laugh loudly as before and rarely came to visit.

Chapter 5
The Give Away

Koshary Women's Quarter on the left

Renie missed the bustle at Nana's, the lively family visits, the laughter of her cousins, the hide-and-go-seek and other games they had played in Nana's big garden.

Why did they leave? Where did they all disappear?

Then Papa went to town, to buy some food, and did not come home. When Renie asked her mother why everybody was leaving them, she was told that they had all gone to live in town, to a place called the *Koshary*.* Renie did not understand and was sad.

She was also still very weak from her illness and spent a lot of time sleeping. It seemed like it had been a long time until Renie started to feel well again, but she still had that annoying cough she could not control.

She was now living in the cottage with her mother. She helped pick vegetables, collect eggs, and watched the goat being milked. She often wondered if Papa, Nana, and the others were ever coming back. Sometimes a neighbor would visit and sit with Mama—they always whispered, as if sharing secrets, but Renie did not care. She went to bed. She was still very tired from that constant cough she had since she had been ill.

One early morning, a neighbor rushed in and whispered, "The Germans are here, they're searching all the houses, looking for Jews—hide, hide."

There was no time to run to Nana's to hide, so Mama grabbed a pillow pushed Renie and they slid under the big sofa in the living room. Renie did not understand what was happening but she sensed her mother's fear and lay obediently, face down in the pillow.

* The *Koshary*, a former compound of a very large sweets company belonging to a prominent Jewish family, turned into long barracks from which inmates left early in the morning, to work in forced labor camps and returned to at night.

There was dead silence.

Then the door was kicked open. Renie saw a pair of the shiniest, blackest boots standing in the doorway. A harsh voice called out, loudly, "*Raus, Yuden—Raus! Raus, Yuden, Raus!*"

Then the boots moved. They were coming towards them. "*Raus, Raus!*"

They stopped at the edge of the living room, stood motionless, turned, and marched towards the door. At the door, they stood still. It was at that moment that Renie's throat tickled and she coughed. The boots turned around. Renie and her mother were dragged from under the sofa.

Terrified as Renie was, she could not resist those mirror-like boots. Her glance rose up and up. She saw a black uniform, a beautiful pair of blue eyes, and a black SS cap. Renie and her mother were taken to town—to the Koshary.

Chapter 6

Reunion in the Koshary

Now Renie and Mama left their home too. They were reunited with the rest of the family in the Koshary. It was an ugly place. There were big, big red brick buildings. No rooms, no kitchen, no bathroom, just one long, long room with beds and beds and beds!

There was a big stinky hole in the ground outside the long, long room—ugh!

Papa and her uncles were in another big room but the children were together with their mothers.

The children spent their days playing games such as "catch," or "hide-and-go-seek." They ate their daily meal around a bed, they were quite content not to have to take a daily bath, and they even learned to "go" in that stinky hole called a "toilet."

In the evenings there was sometimes a concert in the square between the ugly red buildings. Even Yochi played his violin concerto and all the people cheered and clapped their hands for a long time! Renie was so happy for him that her heart almost burst with pride, and when he came down from the podium she gave him a big kiss. All the people laughed and clapped their hands even harder.

Sometimes there was singing and sometimes there was a play, which the children did not understand. They ran around the square and played catch, then their parents would get angry and send them off to bed.

Papa would come back from "work" late and they would talk with Mama, Nana, and Auntie Genia. It must have been a big secret, really serious, because the children were not allowed to hear.

Children have a super sensitive ear when it comes to eavesdropping. They knew something was going on; they overheard the word "bunker" now and again, but since they did not understand, they soon lost interest and went about their business.

Renie, however, was soon to find out what was going on.

One night, when everybody was asleep, Papa came for them and rushed them out of the Koshary. He quickly pushed them into the back of the car, covered them with blankets, and drove them out of town. After a very uncomfortable ride, the car stopped, Papa opened the door and quickly walked them to a big barn.

There in the barn, a big man with a lamp waited for them, rushed them quietly up a ladder, to the end of the loft, left them some cheese, bread, and milk, and disappeared in a hurry. In the stillness of the night, Renie heard Papa's car drive away.

The big man came back very early in the morning. He brought some freshly baked bread, some cheese, milk, and some apples. He didn't say a word; he just whispered, "Don't go close to the wooden walls or you'll be seen!" and left.

Renie and Mama ate quietly and went back to sleep.

Renie was awakened by the laughter of children. It was afternoon—the sun was still high in the sky—and the children were playing hide-and-go-seek. Renie wanted so much to see, but she was not allowed to go near the wooden planks for fear of being discovered.

She was alone and sad. The last rays of the sun broke through the cracks between the planks and then all was quiet again. It became dark. Night had fallen. The big man brought food, Renie and mama ate, and they settled down for the night.

Renie spent her days in quiet solitude.

Then, one morning, she heard a car drive up to the yard. She heard men's voices shouting. Renie immediately recognized the loud words, because they were speaking a language she understood—it was German.

The door of the barn was forced open and two men in black uniforms, shiny boots, and black caps stood there, legs planted far apart.

Mama whispered in terror, "My God, Pell and Mitas! This is the end of us."

Now Renie had heard the names Pell and Mitas before. She had heard that they murdered children, and she was terrified.

The two men in black looked up towards the loft and one of them shouted, "We know you're hiding up there, come down or I'll shoot you where you are!"

Renie and Mama climbed down from the loft and faced Pell and Mitas. Renie's mother kept her face down; she dared not look at those men, but Renie, as afraid as she was, could not resist looking up. She slowly raised her eyes and met a smiling face, but the cold, steel blue eyes did not smile.

Renie heard the man saying to the other one, "Such a beautiful child, the blonde hair, that pug nose, she can't be Jewish!" It was then that Renie heard herself saying in German, "Mr. Pell, Mr. Mitas, please don't kill me, I want to live."

The man turned to Renie's mother and asked in amazement, "What's this? She speaks perfect German?"

Renie's mother answered, "Yes, her grandmother and I are Austrian. I was born in Vienna."

"Such a pity," the man said, turning to his partner. "Shall we let them live a little longer?"

Renie and her mother were driven back to the Koshary. Their lives had been spared.

Renie was back in the Koshary with her family. She was happy, she played with her cousins and was hugged by Nana again. She felt safe. Renie noticed that there were not as many people as before. There were even more empty beds so that the children no longer needed to crouch two or three in the same bed. When she asked where the people had gone, she was told that they had been sent to another Koshary. Renie was satisfied—now she had a bed all to herself and could sleep in comfort.

In the evenings, Papa would bring goodies. He would bring fruit, sometimes a sausage. A few times he even brought some chocolate. Those evenings they would all gather around Nana's bed and she would divide the goodies and give each person a piece. Those were the best times! The children were happy, and Nana was the queen of the family again. Whatever she said, or did, they listened to her, yet she never scolded them or got angry. Her beautiful azure blue eyes were always gentle. They seemed to say, "My love will protect you and keep you safe."

When the children were in bed, the adults would sit together and make plans. Again and again, Renie heard the word "bunker," and there was another word that kept coming up, "*akcia*."* This word seemed to strike terror when it was spoken, but she had lost interest and usually went to sleep and let the adults take care of things.

Each week there were fewer people in the Koshary. Renie wondered if they too would leave soon.

* *Akcia*, the preparation of the Koshary inmates for deportation or killing by gas or shooting outside town.

She was awakened by her mother one dark night, and was warned not to make a sound. They quietly tiptoed out of the long barracks into the cold night. In the darkness she could distinguish the silhouettes of Nana and her cousins but she was swiftly rushed off into the street where Papa waited with two carriages with horses.

Only Mama, Papa, and Renie climbed in. The other figures climbed into the other carriage.

After a quiet ride, the carriage stopped. They descended and were met by a woman, who hurriedly, in utter silence, walked them to a small barn. She left Mama and Renie inside and locked the barn door behind her.

They were alone. There was some bread, cheese, and fresh milk. They ate the fresh bread with cheese; it was delicious. After they drank some milk, they settled down to sleep. Renie would always remember the smell of the freshly cut hay. She filled her lungs and snuggled happily in it and fell asleep with a smile.

The time in the barn passed slowly. There was nothing to do, no one to play with, and Mama could not talk to Renie, fearing that someone might hear. Then, one morning Renie was awakened by heavy pounding on the barn door and the angry barking of dogs. The heavy wooden door was kicked open. There was a burst of golden sunlight. When Renie's eyes got used to the light, she saw two giant German shepherd dogs on a leash. Two men in black uniforms and black caps entered the barn.

Renie was petrified. The dogs were barking viciously, baring their fangs.

The tall man gave a command and the dogs stopped barking. They sat on their hind legs, with their tongues dripping saliva, waiting.

Renie looked at the men. She recognized the tall, shiny leather boots! These were the high, shiny leather boots that had belonged to the man who had found her in her home, under the bed!

She slowly looked up and saw a pair of steel blue eyes. She recognized them—it was the man who had found her before!

He gave Renie a long look; his eyes seemed to recognize her too. She heard him say, "You, again?"

Renie tried to smile. Did the blue eyes seem to soften a bit, she wondered?

He turned to the other man; they were discussing what they should do.

Then the man with the blue eyes said, "Let's take them back to the Koshary. They'll know what to do with them."

Mama and Renie climbed into the back seat of a jeep, the dogs beside them. Somehow they did not seem as threatening. The two German soldiers sat in front. The jeep sped along the streets, and Renie recognized some of the buildings. There was Kino, the movie theater, and she recognized Auntie Genia's big stone house, but where were the people?

Why were the streets so empty?

Mama and Renie were taken back to the Koshary—back to the stench and long barracks.

This time Nana was not there, and neither was the rest of her family. They were all gone. The long barracks were almost empty. There were no children, only some people in their beds, mostly elderly. They all looked sick.

No children played in the square.

There were no concerts.

Even the sky had lost its blue hue.

Renie's heart ached.

One night, when she cried and asked Papa why everything was changing, why everyone was leaving her, he held her tightly in his arms until she stopped crying and fell asleep.

He did not give her an answer.

Chapter 7
The Kino (Sixth Action)

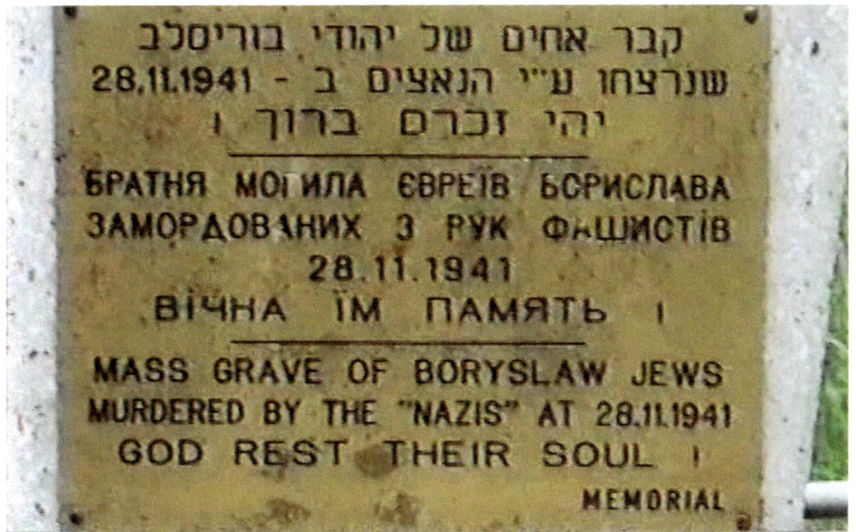

Mass Grave where Most of Renie's family was murdered

One late afternoon, Renie found herself, with Mama and all the people from the Koshary, tightly packed onto a big German lorry. There were soldiers with guns shouting at them, hitting them with the butts of their guns, urging them to climb onto the lorry.

After a short drive, the lorry stopped and they were all forced to get out.

Renie recognized the building—it was Kino, the big theater. They were being packed into the town's only theater. There was hardly any place to stand, it was so full! Renie found it hard to breathe. Mama picked her up and held her in her arms. Now Renie could see. She looked around and saw a sea of frightened faces, some she recognized, some crying. She tried to wave and smile at the familiar ones, but no one seemed to be interested in her.

Then, on the other side of the theater, she caught a glimpse of Nana's loving face. Renie waved at her and Nana smiled in return; she blew a kiss in the air and blinked her beautiful blue eyes. Although she was standing on the other side of the theater, Renie was reassured. Surely Nana would take care of things, as she always did, and this bad dream would pass and they would all be together, and all would be well again.

Around Nana were Auntie Genia, her favorite cousin Yochi, Uncle Zigi, and other cousins. Renie was a little jealous—she wanted to be with them, especially Nana. She asked Mama if they could stand next to Nana, but Mama said, "No!"

Renie started to cry. Mama scolded Renie for crying.

More people were being pushed into the theater. It seemed as if they all became one mass, and no one could even move. Renie was tired and sad. She found it hard to breathe, and it was getting cold. Someone had given Mama a drink for Renie, which she drank, although it tasted horrible. She was too tired to resist. She felt she was being put in a flour sack—she felt warm and relaxed. She remembered yawning. Then she fell asleep.

Renie awoke to the smell of fresh rain in the fields and millions of the brightest stars in the sky. It was the best breath she had taken in a long time! So fresh, so clean.

She realized she was being carried in a sack on someone's back. She whispered fearfully, "Where am I?"

She heard Papa's voice reply," Shh…you are on my back. I'm carrying you, and we're going to a safe hiding place."

"Who's 'we'?" Renie whispered.

"Just Mama and you," was the answer.

"Where's Nana, where's everyone?" she asked.

"After you're safe, I'll go back for the others. Now go back to sleep."

Renie was reassured. She snuggled deeper into the sack and fell asleep with a smile. She was happy.

Renie never saw her beloved Nana or any of her family members again.

Chapter 8
Franciszek and Stefania Maciolek

After Papa left Mama in a "safe" place, he carried Renie to her "safe" place.

She remembered the sound of harsh shrieking whistles and the whoosh of a locomotive. She remembered the strong smell of oil and gasoline, and then the wonderfully fresh smell of fields after the rain.

Papa put Renie down, removed the sack, and very softly knocked on the door of a small cottage. It opened immediately and the smiling face of a farmer bid them to come inside quickly.

It was warm in the cottage and dark. When they were inside, the man lit a kerosene lamp. Renie looked around while Franek—this was the farmer's name—talked softly with Papa. They were in a kitchen with a stove burning softly in the middle. A very pleasant aroma of freshly baked bread hit her nostrils and she suddenly felt very hungry.

The farmer's wife, Stefa, came into the kitchen and quietly put some freshly baked bread, cheese, and warm milk on the table. This was a feast! Renie ate and drank until she was full.

Papa had some food too, but the farmer and his wife just sat and watched in silence.

Then Papa whispered to Renie. He told her she would be staying with the Maciolek family until it was safe to take her home. He hugged her and she clung to him as if she could be absorbed into his leather coat, which he always wore. It had such a reassuring smell—it was the "safest" place.

He promised to come and visit her as soon as he could and swiftly left. The wooden door shut behind him.

Renie was alone, in a strange place with strangers. She felt an unfamiliar ache in her heart and her eyes filled with tears. Franek and Stefa tried to comfort her, gave her a cube of sugar, and gently led her to another room. It was a pleasant room. It had an agreeable smell of freshly washed laundry.

Although the light was dim, Renie could distinguish a girl, somewhat bigger than Renie, sleeping in a bed. Against another wall there was a large wicker basket, which was to become her "safe" place.

Renie was very tired after her long night. She did not object when Stefa dressed her in a pair of somewhat large pajamas and put her to sleep at the bottom of the basket. It was rather pleasant. It smelled of fresh linen and gave her a feeling of protection.

Renie soon fell asleep.

Chapter 9
Annia

Renie woke to an unfamiliar face staring at her. It belonged to a girl with blonde pigtails and blue eyes. The face did not smile; instead, it had a curious look that was somewhat threatening. Later Renie learned that this was to be her older "half-sister," Annia. She was taller and heavier than Renie. She made it clear, right away, that she was the only daughter in this house.

Although it was very early in the morning, the whole family had freshly baked bread, cheese, and milk for breakfast. It was delicious.

After breakfast, Renie was taken aside by Franek and told that, from now on, he was to be her uncle, Stefa was to be her Auntie, and Annia was to be her half-sister.

Now Renie found it very hard to understand that Annia was only half a sister—which half? Annia had two feet, two hands, and she was bigger than Renie, but she did not ask any questions, hoping that she would be told which half was to be her sister.

Uncle Franek then explained to Renie that when they were away from home, she would have to stay in her "safe" place, so that if anyone looked through the shutters they would think that there was nobody home.

Renie was not to be seen! (She later learned that if she had been seen by anyone, the whole family would have been shot.)

Then "half-sister" Annia went to school, Uncle Franek and Auntie Stefa went to work in the fields, and Renie was put in her "safe" place, the bottom of the wicker basket. But it was not the same as it had been at night. A little above her there was another part of the basket. It was filled up to the top with linen. It gave off a lovely fresh smell. Renie lay in her "safe" place and waited.

In the evening, when her new "family" came home, Uncle Franek took her out of her "safe" place and she was allowed to stay up, play with some toys, and then they all had supper together.

Soon after supper, it was bed time. Renie was back in her "safe" place, this time without the linen basket on top. It was quite comfortable. Renie lay awake for a long time thinking about her parents, her real parents, Nana, her beloved cousin Yochi. Her heart ached, her eyes filled with tears, and she cried quietly so no one would hear.

She cried herself to sleep.

Renie got used to her life, even though her half-sister Annia was often a little mean to her. Sometimes she didn't allow

Renie to play with her toys, and sometimes she took the best bits of food from her plate when Uncle Franek worked late in the fields and had his supper later, alone.

Once, when she tried to complain to Auntie about Annia, she got a slap on her cheek. "Isn't it enough that we all put ourselves in danger for you, share what little food we have—you dare lie?"

Renie learned not to complain. Sometimes, when she was still hungry after supper, she would hide a piece of bread under her palate and go to sleep. When she awoke hungry at night she sucked on the bread and felt less hungry.

One evening, just when she was getting ready to go to sleep, there was a knock on the door. Auntie Stefa caught Renie and ran to the room, put her in the "safe" place, put the other half of the basket on top, and signaled to Renie to keep her mouth shut: "Shhhhhhh."

She closed the door and went back to the kitchen. Renie was absolutely quiet; she hardly breathed. She heard the kitchen door open and then she heard a faint voice that she recognized—it was Papa!

Papa had come to visit her, just like he promised!

Renie was allowed to leave her "safe" place and go to the kitchen. She rushed into Papa's arms and clung to him, burrowing her face into his leather coat and taking in the scent that was so familiar to her. He hugged her and kissed her on her head until she pulled back and looked at him. When she finally lifted her face, she saw that the kitchen table was full of goodies. There was fruit, chocolate, candy, and two sausages. Her mouth began to water. That night she went to bed happy and full.

Life went on. Papa came often and always brought plenty of good things to be shared with the whole family. Mama also came to visit, but less often.

Renie got used to her life at the Maciolek farm. She still kept a piece of bread in her mouth at night, just to be on the safe side. It gave her a feeling of security.

Her parents came less often. Annia and Auntie Stefa were less nice to her, now that Papa could not bring goodies anymore. Only Uncle Franek did not change. He was always nice. He would even sometimes stroke her head gently until she fell asleep.

Chapter 10
Borscht

One night Renie woke up very hungry. She had had a small supper, she had swallowed her "security" bit of bread, and she was still hungry. Since her basket was open at night, she climbed out and very quietly tiptoed to the larder to look for something to eat. There was no bread or cheese, no fruit; the only thing she saw was a big pot of borscht, covered by a thick layer of fat. Renie was hungry enough to dare taste a bite. It was awful. She almost spat it out, but her upbringing would not allow her to, so she swallowed the fat. She had another couple of bites and was no longer hungry. She tiptoed back to her "safe" place and went to sleep.

She awoke with a terrible stomachache. It was daylight! Her basket was closed. She could not get to the toilet. Her cramps got worse, and then her bowels gave way, she had no control over them.

Auntie Stefa came home first, and when she opened Renie's basket, she almost collapsed.

Renie had never received such a beating. Auntie Stefa lost all control and beat Renie mercilessly. While she was letting out her anger on Renie, she kept yelling, “Shut up, or I’ll kill you myself!”

Renie never left her basket at night again.

Chapter 11
Uncle Franek's Supper

The borscht incident was never mentioned, and somehow Renie felt a little more empowered. She dared to look at Auntie Stefa and was a little less afraid of her, a little less intimidated by her. She had never told a soul about that night—she was ashamed of what had happened to her more than she was afraid of Auntie Stefa.

Auntie Stefa, on the other hand, was puzzled by Renie's behavior and paid even less attention to her. She did not speak to her unless she had to and there was even less food than before on Renie's plate. Renie often went to bed hungry, and sometimes she cried herself to sleep, but she never thought of telling anyone. Her secret was a double-edged sword. Auntie Stefa was ashamed too. Renie had discovered a secret weapon.

Weeks passed. It was the end of summer, and Uncle Franek often worked late in the fields. When he got home, there was always a plate of hot food waiting for him. Renie could smell the wonderful aroma of meat with potatoes and it made her mouth water.

It was on one such evening that she sat at the table and watched Uncle Franek as he started eating his meal. He smiled at her and asked if she had had her supper. She nodded and told him that she had eaten bread, cheese, and milk for her meal.

He then asked her if she wanted to taste his food. Now Renie was dying to taste that delicious smelling food, but she was afraid to. What if Auntie Stefa saw her? She shook her head sadly.

Franek looked at her for a long time, and then said, "Come here and sit with me. Sit on my lap and eat with me."

Renie could not resist. She sat on his lap and delved her spoon into that delicious dish. She ate and ate and by the time she lifted her head, the plate was almost empty. She was terrified by what she had done. She looked back at Uncle Franek, but he just raised his eyes, patted her on the head, and said, "Now, that wasn't so bad."

That night she fell asleep satisfied.

She was awakened by screams coming from the bedroom. It was Uncle Franek's voice shouting at Auntie Stefa. "Don't you have any decency at all? You took their gold, you took their money, and you starve their child!" Then she heard a loud slap and Uncle Franek's voice again, low and threatening: "If I ever catch her hungry again, I'll, I'll…." Then a door slammed, and Renie could hear no more. She went back to sleep.

The next morning, when Auntie Stefa gave Renie her breakfast, there was a strange look in her eyes. When Renie looked up, she saw a blue bruise on Auntie Stefa's face.

Chapter 12
Life on the Farm

Life with the Macioleks settled into a routine.

They all got up at dawn, took care of their needs, and had breakfast together. Then, Uncle Franek went to his "job" in the fields, Auntie Stefa took care of the house, Annia got ready for school, and Renie cleaned up and made her "bed."

Before Auntie Stefa left to help Uncle Franek in the fields, Renie got into her "safe" place, Auntie Stefa covered it with the linen basket on top, closed and fastened the lid, and the day began.

In her "safe" place, Renie had her rag doll and a drawing book with some crayons.

She kept herself busy. She loved to draw and color in her drawing book, even though there was not enough light. This was her favorite way to pass the time.

Then she got tired and fell asleep.

Auntie Stefa came home, opened Renie's basket, and gave Renie a glass of fresh, warm milk. Renie got used to the taste and rather liked it. It had a funny smell at first—she was told it came from a nanny goat. It was warm, and sweet, and it had a delicious foam on top.

When Annia came home from school, they had lunch. They had soup and vegetables with bread. Sometimes there was chicken and once in a while a piece of meat. They always had a glass of milk with lunch.

Although Annia always had a bigger piece of chicken or meat, Renie learned to accept it. In the beginning, she once asked how come she always received such a small portion. She was told that Annia had to walk to school, study, and walk back home, so she needed more food.

Renie could always have some more bread.

When Uncle Franek came home, he always had a big plate of hot food and the girls had cheese, eggs, bread, and milk.

Sometimes Uncle Franek looked at Renie, as if to check whether she was still hungry, but Renie never made that mistake again.

On Sundays, when the family came back from church to have lunch together, there was always tension in the air. What if a neighbor decided to pop in?

Were it to happen, the family was ready to jump into action.

Renie's basket was prepared, her food would be added to Uncle Franek's plate, her glass removed before anyone opened the door.

Luckily, this did not happen too often.

They lived in a cottage in the middle of Nanna's wheat fields, close to the railway station. It was a long, long walk from anywhere. It was late autumn, and the days were getting shorter.

Renie missed her own family. She often thought about them. Where were they? Were they in hiding like she was? Did they have food? Were they warm?

The next time that Papa came to visit, she would have to remember to ask him.

The trouble was that when he did come, she was so excited that it would always get to be late at night and she would have forgotten all about her question.

Little did she know that she would never get a chance to ask this question.

Chapter 13
Papa's Last Visit

One rainy night, Papa came to visit. He brought sausages, chocolate, and fruit. It was a real celebration! Everybody had some goodies, and they were all in such a good mood.

Papa and Uncle Franek sat and talked for a long time; they talked quietly, like two friends, and they even drank some vodka.

When Renie felt tired, Papa took her to her "safe" place, but she refused to let go of him. She clung to him, her little hands around the back of his head, her nose buried in his chest. She was cold. He covered her with his leather coat and remained with her until she finally fell asleep.

She woke up the next morning wrapped in Papa's leather coat. It had his smell and Renie held it tight in her little arms, buried her nose in it. Tears filled her eyes, and her little heart ached.

The days became shorter, the nights became colder, but Renie had Papa's coat to hold onto. It made her feel safe.

Winter turned into spring, the snow melted, there was more sunshine. Renie remembered when she walked in her garden and smelled the first lilies of the valley last spring and she felt pangs of pain in her heart. Now she was not allowed to go outside. She was so lonely. She so needed to touch the melting snow, to smell the fresh air!

Papa had not come to visit for so long, not since that night when he left her his coat, and there had been no word from him.

One day, Uncle Franek returned from town, where he had gone to buy seeds. He looked different; he seemed sad. That evening, they ate supper in utter silence, and when they finished he gave Renie a hug and patted her on the back of her head. This was quite unusual.

Renie was confused.

Some days later, when Renie asked Uncle Franek if he knew why her parents had not come to visit for so long, he said that her mother could not come because she was on the Russian "side," and her father had been taken by the Germans to the German "side."

Renie could not understand. What did it matter which side they were on? Was this why they couldn't come visit her? She missed them so. If they only knew how much, they would change sides and come to see her.

Time passed, and nothing seemed to change.

Then one day, Uncle Franek came in from working in the fields in the middle of the day. His eyes were bluer than the sky—they smiled! He caught Renie up in his arms and danced her around the room. "The Russians are finally turning things around! They will beat the hell out of the Krauts!" he shouted.

Renie was happy for Uncle Franek, but for the life of her couldn't imagine why Russians turning things or beating the hell out of cabbages made him so happy.

She had never seen him so excited.

Days and days passed and nothing in Renie's life changed.

She still spent many hours of the day in her "safe" place, but somehow it seemed less roomy, less friendly. She found it just a little too tight, and none too cozy. Renie was growing.

Her only consolation was the coat. It had Papa's smell and Renie huddled inside it and felt reassured. She fell asleep and dreamed of home, beloved Nana, and wondered where she was.

Sometimes she dreamed of her family, the way they were all so happy, playing in Nanna's orchard in the summer.

When she woke from a dream, she felt sad. There was a feeling of longing in her stomach, her eyes would fill with tears, and she would cry until she fell asleep again.

Renie developed an attachment to Papa's coat and whenever the feeling of loneliness came over her, she would find consolation in it.

It was now autumn, and she wore that coat most of the time.

She even had it on in the evenings when playing with her rag doll. As time passed, she had more and more need for it; she needed its protection. She needed to remember the smell. It always reminded her of Papa's promise, that one day he would come for her and take her home. She lived with that promise.

Chapter 14
The Surprise Visit

Autumn was over, and a cold winter was soon at its heels. The snow began to fall early, and a bitter cold accompanied it. It snowed and snowed.

Uncle Franek spent much more time inside the cottage now that there was no work in the fields. It made Renie happy to be around him. Sometimes, when Auntie Stefa wasn't watching, he would give Renie an extra piece of dried fruit; when he did, he winked at her, and they exchanged a quick smile. Renie had an accomplice!

She learned to love this man with big, rough hands and unruly hair. He never bothered to comb his hair when he came inside and took off his woolen cap. His face was wrinkled and he looked tough, but when he smiled his blue eyes lit up the room. There was a quick mischievous smile in them, and he looked quite boyish.

Winter set in. It was snowing. The days were short and the nights longer. Renie was happier, for she had Uncle Franek at home to protect her.

By now, Renie's rag doll had lost an arm, and her eyes, which were little buttons, had long lost their color. The doll's head was falling to the side.

Renie asked Uncle Franek if he could fix her doll. He took it from her, held the poor doll in his hands, and asked Renie, "How would you like a nice wooden doll? I have the time now. I can carve one especially for you!"

Renie's eyes lit up. Now her poor doll would have a friend. She said, "Yes."

They were sitting in the kitchen. The fire in the stove gave off a pleasant warmth. Uncle Franek chose a small log from the pile of firewood, turned it in his hand, took his carving knife from his pocket, and sat down across from Renie. He began to peel the bark off the log.

As Uncle Franek worked, Renie watched. She was fascinated. The log started losing chips of wood and some sort of shape began to appear. She could not take her eyes off it.

There was a soft knock on the door.

Renie was immediately swept off to her "safe" place, and the top of the wicker basket was put in place. It was then that she noticed that her old rag doll had been left behind—it was lying on the kitchen table!

Renie held her breath. She concentrated on the sounds coming from the kitchen.

After a while, she heard the door to her room open. There were footsteps. She heard the top of the wicker basket open, then the top part was removed. She kept her eyes tightly shut.

It was then that she heard a soft whisper. "*Reniusiu, to ja, to mama.*"*

Renie opened her eyes. She couldn't believe it—it was Mama! She had almost forgotten that voice. That evening they had supper together. There were so many questions Renie wanted to ask, but most of all she wanted to be held in Mama's arms.

Auntie Stefa had given Mama and Renie Annia's bed so they could spend some time together. They were both given fresh pajamas. Renie soon fell asleep in her mother's arms. She had not been so happy for a long, long time.

They awoke to Uncle Franek shaking them rudely. "The Germans are coming, you have to leave or we'll all be shot." He opened the window leading to the railway station and helped Mama and Renie out. "Go to the station and hide in the latrine. I'll come and get you when it's safe."

Then he closed the window behind them.

Renie found herself knee deep in snow. Mama picked her up and ran with her towards the railway station. There was a train standing on the tracks; it was panting and spewing steam. There were some German soldiers too. Mama ran all the way to the latrine.

They got in unnoticed. Once inside, Mama held the piece of string that was used to hold the wooden door shut tightly in her hand.

* "Renie, it's me, it's Mama."

The train's locomotive was getting restless. It belched a cloud of steam a couple of times, tugged its heavy cargo several times, let off a couple of steam coughs, its whistle shrieked, and it started to haul the wagons forward. It was a laborious effort at first, but with each tug it gained a little more smoothness, until finally it was on its way.

It was soon out of sight. There was utter silence.

Renie began to shiver. She was so cold that her teeth began to chatter. Mama took her in her arms and held her tightly to warm her up. While Renie watched the train through a crack in the wooden door, she had been too excited to be afraid or to feel the cold.

The platform was empty. There were no more trains.

Renie could feel that Mama was getting cold too. She hugged her as tightly as she could and told her that she loved her. She told her that Uncle Franek would come for them soon, that all would be well again. Then they heard tired, shuffling footsteps coming towards the latrine. Mama held on to the string even tighter as Renie looked through the crack. "It's an old man in a German uniform," she whispered.

Mama leaned back to get a better grip on the string. There was a knock on the wooden door and a man's voice asked in German, "Is that you, Hans?"

Renie heard Mama say in a low voice, "*Ja,*" and then give a hefty cough. There was a mumble outside and the tired feet shuffled away. Through the crack Renie saw the old man urinate into the cold wind.

It felt like they waited in the latrine forever. It was even getting a little lighter in the east. At last they heard a familiar voice whisper, "It's me, Franek. Let go of the door."

When the wooden door opened, Uncle Frank took Renie in his arms and covered her with blankets. He put a thick sheepskin coat on Mama and led them back to the cottage. Inside, Auntie Stefa waited for them with hot milk and food.

When Mama finally put Renie to bed, just before leaving, Renie put her little hands around Mama's neck and whispered, "You'll see, everything will be all right, don't worry. I'll take care of you."

Before falling asleep, she felt a little stronger. After all, hadn't Mama left the Russian side just to come to visit her?

The cold winter went on and on. Uncle Franek made Renie a nice doll from white wood. It was so smooth, so pleasant to touch. Auntie Stefa knitted some clothes for the new doll. She even fixed the rag doll's head and sewed on her hand. Renie was happy—now her rag doll had a friend, and now there were two companions to play with and they were all hers!

Nothing unusual happened during the rest of that winter. The "family" went to church every Sunday and there was a special dinner, usually chicken. Renie would eat well that day.

Annia did not dare take food off Renie's plate under Uncle Franek's watchful eyes.

Sometimes after dinner a neighbor would pop in and stay a while. On those occasions, the whole family sprang into action. Renie ran to her "safe" place, followed by Uncle Franek. He covered the top of her basket, and Auntie Stefa and Annia cleared the dishes and quickly sat at the table and "played" cards. Uncle Franek joined them, filled his pipe, and "discussed" men's business. The men always had a drink or two of vodka.

Renie feared and hated these Sundays. She felt cheated; it was her best day of the whole week, and she had so waited for it!

The basket was getting less and less comfortable. Renie felt cramped and had to lie on her side; there was no room to stretch her legs. There seemed to be less air too, and she found it hard to breathe.

Chapter 15
Liberation

Mama had not come to visit for a long time. Renie missed her.

When she asked Uncle Franek why Mama had not come to visit, he told her that there was fighting between the Russians and the Germans, and that it was too dangerous to come and visit.

Renie noticed that Uncle Franek did not seem afraid when he said that. He had a rather proud look in his eyes. She wondered why, and she soon found out.

One morning she was awakened by a terrible noise outside, and it was getting louder and louder. She tried to hide deeper in her basket to shut out the noise. Just then Uncle Franek came into the room, took her in his arms, walked with her to the kitchen door, and opened it!

It was a frightening sight! The noise outside was even louder. It came from big, ugly, frightening machines that crawled forward with a deafening noise. Inside each one was a soldier in a very dirty, sandy uniform. Each one seemed to be driving a monstrous machine.

Uncle Franek cheered, shouting in Russian, “Go, boys, go! Give them hell!”

It was then that Renie noticed there were other farmers following the ugly machines, which she later learned were called tanks. Everyone was cheering, laughing, embracing one another, even dancing. She had never seen such a sight! She was caught up in the spirit of rejoicing. She raised her arms and shouted with the others, at the top of her voice.

“Long live Russia! Long live Stalin! Long live freedom!”

Women ran after the tanks, showering the soldiers with flowers. Some younger women even jumped on the tanks and kissed the soldiers.

Everyone was drunk with victory, and everyone was friends with everyone.

The tanks were followed by soldiers on foot. They were also covered with dust, grease, and sweat, but nobody minded. People ran towards them, hugged them, kissed them, and called them brothers.

Renie never forgot that day. They called it the day of liberation from the Nazi oppressor.

After the tanks and soldiers were gone, all the people returned to their homes. The family went inside. They were all so happy. Uncle Franek put a bottle of vodka on the kitchen table, Auntie Stefa put some fresh baked bread and pieces of bacon out, then the door opened and their nearest neighbor came in.

Renie froze. She had been "caught."

The two men jumped into each other's arms and danced around the kitchen. It was then that Uncle Franek noticed Renie standing there.

He gently walked towards her, lifted her in his arms, hugged her, and explained that the war was over. In a reassuring voice, he said that the Germans had been defeated, that from now on, they were all free, that she no longer needed to hide from anyone. She could go where she pleased.

Her day had come.

Chapter 16
The New Family

From the day of her "liberation," Renie slept in a bed, just like Annia.

She no longer had to hide. She was free to play wherever she wanted.

She could go outside, feed the chickens, watch Auntie Stefa milk the cow. She could even play with the nanny goat. Hadn't she helped Renie when she was sick? After all, wasn't it a nanny goat that had saved her life? She never quite understood how.

When Renie went to sleep in her bed at night, she looked at her "safe" place with mixed feeling. She was comfortable in her new bed—she could stretch her body, turn around—yet she had a strange feeling of longing. She missed the smell of freshly washed linen, the protection it had given her.

There were nights when Renie dreamed of Nana, smiling at her, as she had always done. She dreamed of the long, dark room at the Koshary, of the big German shepherd dogs about to attack her, of Papa coming in through the door with his hands stretched out, coming to take her, of Mama in the latrine holding onto the string. She even dreamed of Yochi playing his violin and everybody cheering him on.

She woke up from these nightmares in terrible fear, covered in sweat and tears. When she was fully awake and looked around, she found herself in her new bed, saw her "safe" place, and was comforted.

She covered herself with her father's leather coat and went back to sleep.

Days passed. Life became more friendly. She learned to enjoy her newfound freedom, especially now that the days were becoming longer and warmer.

Uncle Franek was even more gentle with Renie than ever. He called her "my little orphan"; she loved this unruly man and was happiest when she was around him.

Uncle Franek often spoke of the "family" at the dinner table on Sundays, when the family spent time together, especially when Annia got angry at Renie and call her a "brat."

Even Auntie Stefa was less strict. Sometimes she took Renie's side and said, "Now, girls, get along—no more fighting, the war's over."

Renie had a more active part in the "family" now. She had chores to do, like the rest of the family, she had responsibilities, she even rode to town on days that Uncle Franek needed to go there for "business."

When they met other farmers in town and they asked about Renie, he said that she was his niece, that his brother-in-law had been killed on the Russian front and the child was an orphan. It seemed good to be an orphan—people were nice to her, they gave her a piece of fruit or candy, looked at her with kindness, quite often they patted her on the head and said, "Such perfect Slavic features."

Renie had no idea what this meant but it must have been good to have "Slavic" whatever, because people smiled and were kind to her.

When riding back home with Uncle Franek, she asked why he had told people that she was his sister's child. He answered that it was better this way, that people would not ask too many questions.

"Uncle Franek," she asked, turning toward him," why is it not good to ask questions?"

He gave her a long look and a broad smile slowly spread over his face. He hugged her and said, "Now we are family, and we will have a good life together."

Life on the farm went on. Everyone had a part to play and things were quite pleasant. Summer had come and with it, flowers and fruit on the trees. The vegetable patches were plentiful with cucumbers, tomatoes, and other vegetables.

It was usually Renie's job to pick the vegetables for supper. She loved it—she decided what they would have that evening, and she felt important in her family. She was happy.

Renie was growing up. This was her last summer vacation. In the fall, she would go to kindergarten. Like Annia, she would get an "education."

One day Auntie Stefa asked Renie to help her pick beans for the casserole. They went together to the fence at the end of the field. Renie saw the tall beanstalks heavy with beans and froze. Where had she seen this before? The tall beanstalks laden with bean pods? Then she remembered—it had been in her garden, outside their little cottage, under the window where Papa had slept.

She remembered Nana saying, "Thank God the beans grew high this summer."

Suddenly she remembered!

She had another family: Nana, Auntie Genia, Yochi, Papa, Mama—what happened to them? Where were they? Renie decided not to ask any more questions. She was confused as it was.

Things became more peaceful that summer.

The girls grew closer. They shared their chores, had a lot of laughs together, and sometimes Annia even shared a secret with Renie. Renie sometimes wondered, was Annia still her "half-sister"?

Chapter 17
The Separation

It was towards the end of summer when, one morning, Mama appeared.

She looked strange. She was very thin and her eyes were smaller than Renie remembered. Her hair had been cut very short and it was stringy, not at all nicely arranged as it had always been.

Renie knew this was her mother but she seemed to be a stranger.

When she called out to her daughter to come and give Mama a hug, there was a slight hesitation. Something held the child back.

When Renie did get close to Mama, she was hugged and kissed, but there was something missing. There seemed to be no joy in her heart.

They all sat for a long time at the kitchen table and talked and talked. The girls soon lost interest and went outside to play. From the garden they could hear Auntie Stefa's raised voice. She seemed to be very upset about something, but the girls could only make out the words "You can't take her away now!"

The adults were at it for some time. The girls had lost their curiosity and went on with their own business.

It was getting close to lunch time and the girls felt hungry. They decided to go inside and get something to eat. When they came inside, Auntie Stefa was already making lunch. She was cutting the vegetables as if she meant to kill them—the knife came down again and again with a bang! She was not in a good mood.

Mama was sitting with Uncle Franek and talking quietly. Her eyes were red. She had been crying.

The family and Mama sat down to lunch. Uncle Franek sat at the head of the table, as he had always done. Auntie Stefa sat next to Annia, which was not usual, and Renie sat next to Mama.

Every once in a while, as they ate, Mama put her arm around Renie and squeezed her arm, as if to "feel" her daughter's closeness.

Renie, on the other hand, although she cuddled close to Mama, felt a sadness and she didn't know why. She should have been so happy, she had so longed for and dreamed of Mama's return, and yet….

Mama spent the afternoon with Renie. She talked to her about the family, about how they would start a new life together, how they were now free to do whatever they pleased.

But why couldn't Renie feel happy? There was a gnawing sadness in the pit of her stomach, like a distant pain.

Mama finally left, promising to come back in a couple of days as soon as she found them a place to live in town.

That night Renie should have fallen asleep with a smile, but for some reason that was not what happened. Renie could not fall asleep. Pictures from her past were rushing through her mind and would not let go! She curled up in Papa's coat, relaxed, and finally fell into a deep sleep.

Renie woke up the next morning with mixed feelings. She had become accustomed to her life with her new "family" and now Mama said that she was going to take her away, to live in town. Did this mean that she would no longer be with her "family," that she would be away from Uncle Franek?

She did not want to lose this family. She did not want to be alone again.

The days passed, and there was no sign of Mama.

Renie was confused!

Hadn't Mama said she would come back in a couple of days? Maybe she had changed her mind? Maybe she was back on the Russian side and could not return.

Then, late one morning, Mama came back with two men in uniform. Renie was startled—who were these men? Why did they bring Mama?

She knew they were not German soldiers. Hadn't Uncle Franek said there were no more German soldiers? That the Russian soldiers had gotten rid of them?

Then she heard them speak Ukrainian.

Mama later explained to her that they were Ukrainian policemen who had come to make sure that Renie was her daughter, before she could take her away.

It was hard to part with her "family." Everybody was sad. The girls hugged each other for a long time. Auntie Stefa brought a small suitcase with Renie's clothes (including Papa's leather coat). She put Renie's wooden doll in her hands and patted her head, wishing her well, and then Uncle Franek came in from the fields.

Renie ran to him as fast as her legs would carry her. She jumped into his arms, put her hands around his neck, and held him tight. She did not want anyone to see her crying. She cried so hard her whole body shook. Uncle Franek held her in his arms and did not let go for a long time.

When Renie finally pulled back and looked at him, she saw tears running down his face.

Chapter 18
The New Beginning

The two policemen drove them to town.

On the way, Renie was excited to see such big, green fields—there were so many trees, a wide river was flowing fast, so full of water that it filled her with wonder.

Her heart beat faster and faster. She did not know where to look. Everything was so new to her. She kept jumping from one window to another. She did not want to miss anything!

The car sped on and soon reached "town."

The streets were paved with white cobblestones. The pavement was higher, it was clean, and every few meters there were tall trees with flower buds on them. Between the trees there were things called "lamp posts"—Renie was told that as soon as it got dark, they would light up so people could see and walk on the streets.

On both sides of the street there were beautiful, high buildings, each one different, with fences that looked like someone had drawn them. There were beautiful flowers in the gardens around each building. Renie wondered if they would live in one of those buildings, but she was too busy looking around to ask.

They continued to ride in the car a little longer and then they stopped in front a small house that was not at all as nice as the ones she had seen. They got out of the car, thanked the policemen, opened the small gate, and walked into their new "home."

It was a small house. There were two rooms with furniture, a big bathroom with a big white tub, a small kitchen with a tiny table and two chairs.

It was not at all what Renie was used to. She was used to a big kitchen with a large stove in the middle of it, which had a fire burning in it all day. She was also used to a nice smell coming from things cooking on that stove. She was used to a very large wooden table with two benches on either side.

In the bedroom there was a huge bed. She ran and jumped onto it. She liked this. She was going to like living in town.

Chapter 19
Living with Mama

Renie and Mama settled down in their new home.

They had some bread. It was not as tasty as the bread Auntie Stefa baked every morning. They ate some sausage, which tasted good, and they had some hot sweet tea and soon settled down for the night.

Of all the things in the new home, Renie loved the big bed best! There was so much space in it. She could roll over and over and still not fall off! When she had enough rolling around, she clung to Mama and fell asleep in her arms. She was smiling.

Renie woke to a sunny, warm day. Mama had already woken up. She was in the kitchen making breakfast. They had breakfast of bread, sausage, and tea, then Mama dressed Renie and they went for a walk.

They walked for a long time until they came to the town.

There were the high pavements again. It was fun to walk on them, especially when Renie walked on the pavement and Mama walked on the cobblestones below. They held hands and laughed.

They reached the town.

The big trees were beginning to blossom and their leaves were opening. The trees were close to one another. She later learned that they were walking along the "boulevard" of the town.

On both sides of the boulevard there were big houses, with their fences and gardens that she had seen the other day when the policemen drove them to town. Now they did not look quite as nice as they had yesterday. The gardens were messy and had a lot of weeds in them; the fences, although beautifully cut, were rusty and their paint was peeling off.

They walked on and then Renie stopped. On one of the tall lamp posts, she saw a body hanging. She was horrified! She found it hard to breathe. It was the body of a young woman. She was dead.

She looked like her broken doll had looked, before she had been fixed. The head was tilted, arms and hands hanging at her sides. Renie squeezed her mother's hand, looking up to her face, waiting for an explanation. Her mother told her that this woman had been a bad person, that during the war she had been a "collaborator," that she had helped the Germans find Jews and other people and kill them, or send them to the death camps.

When the Russians won the war, they punished the "collaborators" by hanging them, so everybody could see what they did to "traitors."

That night, Renie could not sleep. Each time she fell asleep, she dreamed of her doll hanging on the lamp post, swinging in the wind, and she would wake covered in sweat.

The next few days, when asked if she wanted to go for a walk, she found a reason not to go. She either had a stomachache, a headache, or just wanted to sleep.

Finally, she was taken to a doctor. The doctor examined her and said that he could find nothing wrong with her. He then asked her a million questions, after which she said that she was tired and wanted to go home to sleep.

Once she reached home, she had a small meal and fell into a deep sleep. She did not dream that night.

The spring days passed, and Mama and Renie led a peaceful life. They did things together. They tidied the house every day, they went out to the neighborhood store to buy fresh bread, milk, sometimes some sausage and fruit. They spent a lot of time talking together.

Mama told Renie stories about her childhood, Nana, her family, and Renie began to remember things. She "saw" pictures of her family, gathering in the garden, the children running around, laughing, playing, Nana bringing trays of fruit and goodies.

She smiled sadly. It had been a long time since….

One day, when they were sitting on a bench in the park near their home, Renie asked her mother when they were going back to their real home. To Nana, Papa. Auntie Genia, and the others. Her mother's eyes filled with tears. She said that they could not go back, that other people were now living in their home.

"So where do all the others live?" Renie asked.

Mama put her arms around Renie and held her tightly. Renie felt her mother sobbing; her whole body was shaking. Then she heard her mother saying through her tears, "It's only you and me now, baby. That's all there is."

At first, Renie could not quite understand that they were all gone. Gone where? But she was too scared to ask.

Days passed, and it began to dawn on Renie. All her family members were dead. She would never see any of them again. It was the Nazi Germans who had murdered them, or sent them to "extermination" camps to be murdered. How she hated them!

Time was moving along slowly. Mama and Renie settled into a routine. They prepared their meals together, went shopping for food, and went for long walks.

One morning, as they were walking, she started to recognize where they were. Renie realized they were nearing a familiar alley, she recognized the tall trees, which she now knew were called chestnuts. They were in full bloom. Their leaves were very big; they looked like green stars.

Renie also learned that the trees had brown fruit in the autumn, which were called chestnuts too and could be eaten once they were roasted. She was looking forward to the autumn so she could have some.

As they came closer to the center of town, Renie saw several figures hanging on lamp posts. They all looked the same. They reminded her of her broken doll. Then she remembered what Mama had told her. They had been bad people—they helped the Germans "exterminate" all the Jews. They were the ones who had helped kill her family! She felt a wave of anger sweep through her entire body. She hated these swinging bodies; she wanted to kill them too!

Suddenly she let go of her mother's hand and ran as if she were possessed. When she reached a body, she jumped as high as she could and pushed the hanging feet. The whole body swung hard. She then ran on till she got to the next body and pushed that one too. The whole time she kept screaming, "You deserved to die! I'm glad you're dead! I hate you! I hate you!"

As she ran, Renie sobbed and shook like a leaf. She ran from body to body, not looking at who or what it was, jumping as high as she could and pushing with all her might, until each body swung. And she kept screaming, "I hate you, I hate you, you helped the Germans kill Nana, Papa, Yochi…!"

With each push of a swinging body, she added the names of her loved ones and ran on to the next. Finally her mother caught up with her. She held Renie tightly against her breast, not letting go, all the time whispering, "You have me and I have you now, we love each other very much, no one will ever, ever hurt us again." Mama kept repeating it again and again. Renie, however, could not bring herself to listen. She was sobbing so hard; she felt her heart ache so much that she thought it would break.

The whole time she sobbed and her frail body shook like a leaf.

Slowly her tears subsided and Renie heard her mother say, "No one will ever, ever, ever hurt us again!" It took a long time for Renie to calm down. Her mother kissed away her last tears, gently held her hand, and said, "Now we will go home and have some ice cream on the way." With her hand in Mama's, her thoughts moved on. She thought of the sweet ice cream and slowly started to walk back toward their home.

Renie never mentioned that day. No one ever spoke about it.

Chapter 20
Batko Stalin (Big Papa)

Life was good with Mama.

Renie was happy to share the house chores with Mama, take long walks with her, and ask millions of questions, most of which Mama answered. Mama knew so much about the family. Renie learned so many things about Nana, that her husband, Grandpa Baruch, was in the war and never came back, that Nana alone "brought up" her family. Renie did not quite understand what it meant to "bring up" a family, but she did not want to stop the story to ask. Some of the stories she remembered, but some were new to her. She loved the stories—it was as if her loved ones were alive. Renie pictured the different faces, their smiles, and sometimes she even thought she heard Yochi playing the violin concerto he had played in the ghetto. How proud she had been when all the people clapped their hands after his performance!

She never tired of listening to the stories. Although her mother tried to read some children's stories to her, she always led her back to her favorites, the ones about their life with her family, their home, and especially the one's about Nana.

Mama never took walks to the alley again. They walked in other directions, to the fields outside town where they gathered wildflowers and special "red seeds" from which Mama brewed red tea—it was red and nice. Summer was coming to an end, the days were getting shorter, and their walks were shorter too. When they came home from their walks, they made supper together. Mama taught Renie how to brew tea, set the table, and fold the napkins. Renie enjoyed being a little housewife. When they finished eating supper each evening, Renie asked Mama to tell her favorite stories. "Again?" Mama said, but Renie would beg, "Please, please tell the one about...."

Sometimes Mama told Renie about school, how it was time that Renie started kindergarten, how children from town came to play in class, how they sat with a teacher and learned to draw, write, and read, how they played games together. But Renie was afraid that when she went to school and Mama left her there, she would never come back, just like everyone else who had left her. She would be alone again. She would not go to school! She would not leave Mama.

For some time, Mama did not mention school again. Renie was relieved. No school for her. They continued their daily walks, most of which were in town—however, when Renie asked where the flowers had gone, Mama explained that they were getting ready for the long winter sleep so that next summer they could bloom again.

Renie understood. She accepted the idea that the earth needed to sleep in the winter so it could wake up in the spring and bloom again. She remembered Auntie Stefa's garden, where the flowers and vegetables went into the ground for "a long sleep."

One day, as they were taking their walk to town, Renie noticed a colorful playground with swings and carousels—they were so inviting that Renie wanted to play, but the playground with its nice little house was surrounded by a fence with a gate that was closed. Renie asked Mama why the playground was closed, and Mama answered that the playground was the school— that children would come to play next week.

"Can I come to play next week?" Renie asked.

"Yes, of course," Mama said. "It is open to all children."

Renie was excited. She would love to play in the kindergarten—but what was "next week"? That night, Renie went to sleep happy. She had great expectations for what the morning would bring. Finally, the morning came. Renie put on her "bestest" dress, Mama tied her hair with a bow, gave Renie her hand, and they proudly walked out the door hand in hand.

Renie had not eaten breakfast that morning; she was too nervous to eat. Together they walked to town. After some time they reached the school. Renie's excitement grew. She could not wait to go inside the school.

This time the gate was open. Renie walked inside. There were no other children. The path to the schoolhouse was long and winding. Renie squeezed Mama's hand to get reassurance that it was all right. They reached the threshold of the school; there was a long corridor that ended in a wall with an enormous painting of a man in a green uniform, a green cap with a golden star. He had a very big smile, and his hand was pointing down towards a large table filled with sweets, cakes, and chocolates. Renie was overwhelmed! She bashfully asked Mama who the man in the picture was. "Why, that is *Batko* (Papa) Stalin, father of all Russia!"

Renie suddenly remembered Russian soldiers in tanks. She had been "set free" by Russians. How they smiled and hugged her—they had sung all the way to the "front," although she never understood what front? Where was it? Renie's heart was suddenly filled with an incredible longing, a feeling she could not understand…a feeling of sadness? So this man, with such an open smile, was the father of all these soldiers? She loved him. She loved *Batko* Stalin! Renie stood by the table full of sweets. She was tempted to take one but did not dare.

When she finally got the courage to ask Mama if she could take one, a nice tall lady came towards them. She had a beautiful smile. When she reached them, she stretched out her hand to Mama and said, "I am the teacher. My name is Natalia." She then turned to Renie and asked, "And what is your name, you lovely child?" She reached out her smooth, cool hand, which Renie hesitatingly took.

"Renie," she replied quietly.

"I like it very much," the teacher replied. "Renie, would you like some chocolate? Help yourself."

Renie stretched out her hand to take a piece. To do this, she had to lift her face. She saw *Batko* Stalin looking at her with a kind smile, giving her his permission. The chocolate was delicious. It was the first piece of chocolate she had eaten since leaving Uncle Franek's house, when Papa used to bring goodies to share, including chocolate. She was going to like school after all!

Life was good. Mama helped dress Renie and comb her hair every morning, and they both set off, Renie to school and Mama to work. When she arrived at school, she was greeted by her teacher Natalia, whom she liked very much. The teacher always welcomed her with a smile, asking how she was, wishing her a good morning, but most of all she smelled like a flower. Renie loved her smell. At school they learned to sing songs, in Polish and in Russian, to read and write. They also did exercises in the yard and listened to music and stories, which Natalia read to them. Renie liked to do all these things. When it was play time, the girls all chose dolls to play with. Renie, however, could never choose a doll to play with, so she did not play with the other girls.

Chapter 21
Long Train Ride

One day Mama came to school early, before the children had their breakfast. She spoke to the teacher, Natalia, then she came over to Renie and told her that she was there to take her home. On the way home, Mama explained to Renie that they were going on a trip. They were going by train to another town with other people who, like them, had survived the war.

When they got home, Renie saw two suitcases, which were filled with all their clothes. One suitcase was large; it was Mama's. The other was very small; it was Renie's. Renie was sad to leave her home. She was used to her school, she liked her friends, and above all she loved her teacher, Natalia. She said goodbye to her things, to the wide bed she had shared with her mother, picked up her little suitcase, put on her little student cap, and walked to the door courageously. Although she felt tears filling her eyes, she did not cry, she did not look back. She took Mama's hand and started to walk towards the train station into town.

They walked together in silence. So many thoughts were going through Renie's mind. Where would they go? Would they have a nice wide bed like the one at home? Would there be a nice school with a yard with swings and toys? Would there be a teacher like Natalia? She already missed her home. Her eyes began fill with tears, but she held back her tears; she was not supposed to cry. They came to the train station. There were many people there, mostly old people, but not many children. Each person had a suitcase in their hands, and they stood together not looking around, not speaking. They all seemed to be looking down at their feet. More and more people came to the station—they all looked alike, walking quietly, not looking up. They all wore coats even though it was not cold. Soon the station was packed with people, all standing quietly, waiting. Renie noticed some Ukrainian policemen walking up and down in front of the people, and they were quiet too; they also did not speak.

Then a train whistle was heard, and soon the train slowly came into sight. Within a few minutes it stopped in front of the wall of silent people.

After the train stopped, it gave a loud hiss, then went silent. Some of the policeman pushed open the heavy doors and started to shout and scream at the people to get on the train. Slowly the people started to move towards the train, a few at a time, still only looking at their feet. They did not look at the policemen. Renie, however, did look up at them. They were like the ones who had come with Mama to take Renie away from Uncle Franek and her family. Why were they so angry now? Why were they shouting mean words at them? The people were moving slowly, then one policeman lifted a club and started to hit the people on their heads and shoulders.

There was a cry and the people started to move quickly towards the train, trying to protect themselves from more beating. All of a sudden "all hell broke loose" and the other policemen followed suit and beat the moving "wall" of people mercilessly, all the time shouting and yelling and swearing at the tops of their heads! Mama lifted Renie in her arms for fear of her being trampled. With the rest of the "wall," they were pushed forward to the big, dark hole of the train car. When Mama climbed into it, still clutching Renie tightly, she pushed herself towards a little opening with barbed wire over it, and only then did she let Renie down, as close to the only tiny window as possible. Mama stood behind her, in this way protecting her from being trampled by others.

More and more people were pushed into the train car until they stood like one mass, not able to move. Someone vomited; the smell was awful. Many were crying aloud, especially women, and then the heavy iron door was pushed shut. There was dead silence, occasionally broken by muffled sounds coming from the airtight, packed wagon. Then the train suddenly jerked forward, people lost their balance, but they were yanked like one body so no one was really hurt, just terrified.

There was little air inside the train car. It was completely dark; it was night.

The train was travelling fast now. The swing of each curve swung the people with it. Renie held on to the small opening with one hand and held Mama's tightly with the other. She was getting tired, and she often switched hands. She wanted to sit down on the floor of the wagon, but Mama explained that if anyone saw the place at the "window" they would think it was empty and move towards it, and Renie would find it hard to breathe.

Renie peeked behind Mama. She was used to the darkness now and saw some silhouettes of people. Most of them were standing but some places were empty—were these people sitting on the floor, she wondered?

The smell was so bad that she turned her face back to the window. At least there she could breathe; she smelled the wind and decided that Mama was right!

The train ride continued into the night. The movement of it made Renie sleepy—she felt safe, her hand in Mama's, and closed her eyes for a moment.

She was awakened by the train whistle, and when she opened her eyes it was morning. She looked around her and noticed more people on the wagon floor. They were not sitting; they were asleep.

Then the train stopped completely. Someone called, "Gliwice—everybody out!"

The heavy iron door of the train car opened slowly. People began to move slowly towards the open door. It was then that Renie noticed that the people on the floor were not sleeping; they were dead.

Mama picked Renie up and moved slowly towards the open iron door.

They got off the train.

The fresh air hit Renie's face and she loved it! She breathed deep breaths as if they might be her last. Mama picked up her suitcase and gave the little one to Renie, and they left the train station hand in hand.

Chapter 22
New Home

Mama and Renie followed the people who had been on the train. She remembered some of them. They all walked in the same direction, away from the stinking train car, towards the big gate and out into the street. It was a warm sunny morning. Outside the station, they were met by many people— they were all smiling, everyone who stood in line to greet them gave each person who came off train a sandwich, a bottle of water, and a flower.

Renie asked Mama who these nice people were, and how come they were so nice and happy. She got a shy smile in return, and Mama hugged Renie. They continued walking towards buses that were waiting for them.

After a short ride, the bus stopped at a big house and they got off. Mama picked up her suitcase, Renie picked up her suitcase, and they both walked towards the door.

A smiling lady was standing in the entrance and shook hands with Renie and her mother. She was nice, she spoke to Mama in a soft voice and told her that the apartment was ready. She led them down a few steps and with a key opened the door to a small room, a very small kitchen and a very, very small bedroom. The apartment was dark. There was a window that was high and small, and Renie could see people walking on the street—but all she could see was their feet!

In the living room there was a big table with four chairs, a fireplace, and a small sofa, and in the bedroom there was a cupboard and a bed—but a small one, not at all like the one she was used to.

Renie was disappointed. Where would she put her dolls? Her rag doll that Auntie Stefa had fixed and her wooden doll that Uncle Franek had carved for her, both wearing the dresses that Auntie Stefa had sewed. Suddenly her eyes filled with tears and she felt a pang in her heart. She missed her Uncle Franek. Would she ever see him again?

Mama picked Renie up, held her tightly, and sat on the bed, all the time whispering softly that things would be better, that here they would have peace, that people were nice and they would find a school for Renie. At that moment, Renie burst out crying, "But will Natalia be at this school?"

Renie cried until she fell asleep. She was too tired to care.

She woke up the next morning.

Chapter 23
Life in Gliwice

Renie awoke early in the morning. Mama was in the kitchen making breakfast—bread and warm milk. It was very tasty, and Renie ate it all; she was hungry.

They both sat in the tiny kitchen, and when they finished eating, Renie asked what they were going to do.

Mama answered that they would go for a walk in the new town, to get to know it. Soon they left the house and began to walk. The first place they visited was a small shop, which, like their new home, was lower than the street. The lady in the shop greeted them with a smile, welcomed them to their new home, and explained that the shop had fresh bread every morning, fresh eggs from a farm, fresh milk and butter, also from a farm, vegetables and fruit and anything they needed. Mama thanked the lady and promised to come later to buy what she needed. She also asked the lady where they should go to get to know the town. The lady was happy to help and soon Renie and Mama started their first walk in Gliwice.

The houses were all tall. They didn't have gardens with flowers around them, and they were not as white as the ones at home. Renie asked where the alley with the tall chestnut trees was. She was told that it was a small town, that most people were away all day and didn't have time to walk in an alley; they probably went out during the evening. They walked on in silence until they came to the market place. It was very noisy, people were buying and selling things, and Renie saw live chickens in a box, tiny little yellow chicks. They were so cuddly that Renie's heart went out to them. She so wanted to hold one. The lady who was selling them picked one up and gave it to Renie to hold—it was so soft and chirping happily. Renie loved it, and she asked Mama if she could have one. But she was told maybe some other time, that they had not settled in yet and they had to return to the lady at the store and buy things for dinner. The lady took the baby chick from Renie's hands and threw it in with the others.

Renie almost cried. Her heart ached—poor little chick, did it die? Was it hurt? She stood there watching until she saw it happily playing with its brothers. The lady paid no attention to the chicks and turned to another customer.

Renie and Mama continued their walk. They walked slowly until they reached the little store near their house. At the store Mama bought some food, and they walked back to their new home. Renie went to the bathroom to take a shower and Mama went to the kitchen to prepare their meal.

After they finished eating, Renie went to the bedroom to play with her dolls. When asked if she wanted to hear a story, she said she was too tired, that she preferred to play with her dolls. Besides, the bed was too small for all of them. She soon fell asleep.

When Renie woke in the morning, she could smell a familiar smell—it was the smell of an egg frying in butter. She quickly went to the kitchen and found Mama making breakfast. It was a feast! There was fresh bread that smelled wonderful, cheese, eggs in butter, and fresh milk. When Renie sat down at the table, for a moment she remembered Nana. This smell was just like the breakfasts Nana had made. She was sad and wondered where Nana was? Where was everyone? Were they having breakfast? And then Mama's voice brought her back. "Eat your breakfast before it gets cold."

Later they went for their daily walk.

That day their walk was a little shorter. Renie recognized some of the streets and soon found herself in the market place again. This time it was more familiar; they walked and walked and saw different things for sale, but they did not buy anything.

Suddenly Renie heard Mama cry out, "Fanny, is that you?"

A woman turned around and cried equally loudly, "My god, it's Ella! Is it really you?" Both women fell into each other's arms and in a long hug cried and kissed each other, cried and kissed for a long time.

After they stopped, Mama told Renie that this was Fanny, her best friend from school, that she had also survived!

The two women sat in the market place and talked and cried, hugged, and cried for a very long time.

Renie walked around the different stalls, looking for the little chicks, but she did not find them. When she came back to where Mama was sitting with her friend Fanny, she found them talking and crying, talking and crying.

Fanny had been in Gliwice for some time, and she had much to tell Mama.

There were many "stalls" in the market place. Fanny worked in one where she sold fresh eggs from a farmer. Renie knew what this was. Uncle Franek also sold eggs in a market, she remembered—she could never forget.

That night, before they went to sleep, Renie asked about Fanny. Who was she? Was she a good friend? Did she have a family, a daughter?

Mama tried to answer all her questions, but there were always more. Renie was glad that they had found a friend who, like them, had "survived." Maybe other people had survived and one day they would find them too?

That night, with Mama at her side, Renie fell asleep with a smile.

In the morning, she woke up to a nice breakfast with Mama, who also told her that today they would go to the post office. Fanny told her that all survivors were getting help from America—once a month they got a big box with clothing, food, and other things, and a "check," which meant money, to buy things like fruit, vegetables, and "other" things.

Mama hugged Renie and said, "Didn't I promise you that things would get better? That we would have a good life?"

Renie looked at Mama and smiled—she was happy.

They went to the post office. Mama was asked some questions, then she signed a piece of paper and got a "check." They went to the bank and got money for the "check." Renie immediately asked, "Is that enough money to buy a yellow chick?" Mama just laughed aloud.

She was happy!

Mama and Renie had a new life.

Every morning after breakfast they cleaned the kitchen and bedroom together, got dressed, and went for their walk in town.

They walked in the fields, outside the town, sometimes gathering leaves for their tea, sometimes some potatoes, after the fields were cleared by workers. They went to the market place to visit with Fanny and other market ladies, who by now had become friends.

They talked among themselves about how they survived the war, who had not survived, who were lucky to have money and buy a house and who had a very small apartment, who could afford luxuries and who could not.

By the middle of the day, a few children came to the market place. They came from the school to be with their parents and eat lunch. Later they played games and laughed together. Renie was not asked to join them and she was too shy to try and join, and besides, it was lunch time and she would soon go home and have lunch with Mama.

That day, after they had lunch at home, Mama told Renie that she had some good news. She said that next week was the first day of June, the first day of summer, and they would get their first package from America! They hugged with excitement, although Renie had no idea why they were so excited. But it was so good to see Mama so happy.

That day soon came.

Renie went with Mama to the post office. It was exciting to receive a package - and from America!

They walked outside with a big package. It was heavy; Renie tried to help carry the package until they reached home. Mama put the package on the kitchen table and opened it.

It was full of cans! Soup cans, meat cans, fruit cans, coffee cans, sweet milk cans, and there were also sweets and chocolate. There were also silk stockings for Mama and cream for her face and a small bottle of the "bestest" smelling perfume. It was a dream!

In the evening they had a celebration dinner just like rich people. They could not have been more happy.

That night they both slept well.

In the morning, they went on their daily walk and as usual ended up in the market place.

Mama told Fanny the good news about the package from America. They hugged and smiled happily.

Fanny explained that Mama could exchange some of the

things at the market place and get things she needed more such as chicken, eggs, vegetables. Renie listened carefully to every word but said nothing, although she had not forgotten—she was thinking about her yellow chick.

She smiled to herself.

Fanny, who knew all the survivors in the town, told Mama that there was a very rich family in the town who were looking for a cook. Mama, although she wasn't a real cook, decided to ask for the job. She got it.

Now, three days a week Mama took Renie to the market place to stay with Fanny, and she went to work.

It was nice at the market place. People came to buy food—vegetables, fruit, fish, chicken, meat, and sometimes even flowers.

Renie asked Fanny, whom she now called Auntie Fanny, if she could help. Auntie Fanny was more than happy to have a little helper!

She taught Renie how to sell things, how to speak to people, how to smile at them.

Renie learned the trade very quickly. People were nice to the little blonde girl; they were happy to buy things from her. Auntie Fanny was very happy too. She said that Renie was a "natural" and that she brought in good business.

What was more important was lunch time, when children came from school. They all looked at Renie a little differently. She, on the other hand, felt very important—she was a "saleslady."

When Mama returned from work, Auntie Fanny told her what a good "saleslady" Renie was, that she would have to pay her a salary. They all laughed.

Time went on. Summer vacation came and all the children were free from school. One morning, one of these children came to Auntie Fanny's stall. It was one of the older boys. He turned to Auntie Fanny and said, "My mother sent me to buy six large eggs."

Auntie Fanny, with a smile, said, "Renie will give you six large eggs. She is now a saleslady."

The boy was confused, but he turned to Renie and said in a man's voice, "Six large eggs, please."

Renie was very serious. She went to the egg section, took a paper bag, and chose six of the largest, nicest eggs, put them in the paper bag, and with a smile, gave them to the boy.

He said thank you and turned to Auntie Fanny to pay for the eggs, but she said, "Renie will take the money."

With the coins in his hand, he turned to Renie and asked if she would like to join the group of children to play.

Renie became serious and said, "Thank you, but I have a job."

He turned away and said, "See you."

Renie had won the first battle!

Chapter 24
Mama Goes to Work

Summer was a good time for Renie.

She and Mama took long walks, the weather was nice, Renie had ice cream every day, the town was busy with people and children going to the shops and having picnics in the woods—it was a happy time for all.

They visited Auntie Fanny every day and Renie worked as her helper and even got a salary based on how much money she made selling eggs.

One day a lady came to the market place. She was nicely dressed and wore a big hat. She stopped to buy some eggs and Renie, with a big smile, just like Auntie Fanny had taught her, asked if she could help.

She could not help but notice the looks from the people around her. They were looking at the lady as if she were a queen.

Renie carefully chose twelve eggs, put them in a paper bag, and looked to Auntie Fanny for approval when she said, "That will be fifty groszy."

The lady gave her the money, turned to Auntie Fanny, and said, "That is quite a little helper you have here, and smart too."

Renie was ready to burst with pride!

Then the lady turned to Auntie Fanny and asked if she knew someone who could cook for the family for Shabbat, as her cook had left her. Auntie Fanny said she would ask her friend if she could come and cook for her. The lady thanked them and left with a smile.

When Mama came in the afternoon, Auntie Fanny asked her if she wanted to work as a cook for a very rich Jewish family. Mama stopped to think for a while. "I am not really a cook," she said, "and especially not of Jewish food."

Auntie Fanny laughed and said, "neither is Mrs. Landau."

Mama took the job.

Now Renie went to "work" on Friday mornings and Mama picked her up in the afternoon when she finished cooking for the Landaus. The job of cooking for the family did not make Mama happy. When she came to pick Renie up on Fridays, Auntie Fanny asked her a lot of questions. How was Mrs. Landau? What was their house like? How did Mama manage as a cook? And many more.

After a while, Renie lost interest. She noticed that Mama was tired. When they reached their home, they had a light supper and Mama went to sleep early. There were no stories. When Renie asked how Mama's day was, Mama said, "Ask me tomorrow. I'm too tired to talk." And she immediately fell asleep.

Renie now spent her Fridays alone. She played with her toys, but she felt lonely. She missed the conversations they had at bed time, the stories of her early childhood. These were the times Renie remembered her loved ones—Nana, Yochi, Papa, Auntie Genia, and the rest of the family. She often cried when she heard the stories—they made her sad—but now, in the silence of Friday nights, she missed the pictures of her family. She did not want to forget them, not ever!

The summer was coming to an end. Soon Renie would have to go to school. She was excited but a little worried. She was reminded of her school in the other town, of her teacher Natalia, whom she missed so much. Would she like this big new school? Would she like the teachers? Then she thought of the boy who had bought eggs for his mother. He came every week now and they talked a little. She felt she at least had one friend at the new school.

Renie had other worries on her mind. It was Mama.

She saw Mama every Friday afternoon in the market place when Mama came from the Landaus. She was always so tired. Her hands were rough and red, and when they reached home, she ate very little and went to sleep.

Renie always shut the bedroom door so Mama could sleep while she played in the kitchen, quietly, so as not to disturb her. But sometimes she heard muffled sounds coming from the bedroom. When she went closer to the door, she heard Mama crying. Renie had to think fast. She would not let

Mama cry without doing something about it!

When Sunday came and Renie went to "work," she had a talk with Auntie Fanny. She told her about how tired Mama was, how red and rough her hands were, how little she ate, and above all how she cried in bed, quietly, so Renie would not know how unhappy she was.

That evening, when Mama and Renie were having supper, there was a knock on the door. Mama got up to open the door, there was Auntie Fanny with a basket of fruit and a big smile! She hugged Mama and they both sat down at the table. They all had supper together and spoke about life.

Then Auntie Fanny turned to Mama and asked, "What is wrong with you? You look like hell! Are you sick? Go to a doctor—I'll give you the address of one who is very good, he is nice too, and he lost his wife a year ago." Mama began to cry, and she tried to explain to Auntie Fanny why she was so unhappy. She was ashamed but Auntie Fanny was her only friend.

She cried with Mama when she heard the story. Mr. Landau was a nice man. He went to work on Friday mornings, when Mama came to work, and he always greeted her politely. But Mrs. Landau started cleaning the house as soon as he left. She told Mama she had to clean the whole house before she went to the kitchen to cook Shabbat dinner, that everything had to be ready for Shabbat before three o'clock and Mama had to leave at ten to three, before Mr. Landau came home.

Auntie Fanny left the table and hugged Mama for a long time. They both cried together.

At that point, Renie was too tired and sad to hear any more. She was glad that Mama had a friend who cared. Renie was free to go to sleep.

First day of school

Chapter 25
The First Day of School

The first day of school came on a sunny September day.

Renie was dressed in a blue dress. She had a new lunch bag and a bow in her hair and new shoes.

She was excited. She was happy walking all the way to school. When she entered the school grounds, she was amazed. She had never seen so many children. Some were in first grade, like her, others were bigger, in higher grades.

Then the bell rang and the children arranged themselves into lines according to their teachers' call.

Everybody was quiet, listening for their names to be called so they could get into their lines.

Renie's name was called and she was placed in Class A, one of the first grade classes. When Renie was standing in her line, she could not help but look towards the other lines hoping to find her only friend. She finally saw him waving at her. She bashfully waved back.

When the children were seated in their classroom, the teacher called out each name. The girl or boy whose name was called stood up, and everyone looked at that student and greeted him or her by saying, "Good morning." When Renie's name was called, "Irena," she did not recognize it. She looked around for Irena, but there was silence in the room. Everybody looked around for Irena to stand up. Then the teacher came close to Renie and asked, "Aren't you Irena?"

And Renie said, "My name is Renie."

"Would you like to be called Renie?" asked the teacher.

"Yes, please," Renie answered.

The teacher then called out "Renie" and Renie stood up and everyone said, "Good morning, Renie."

The second battle was won. She had been recognized.

The first day of school was over.

Chapter 26

The Invitation: "Chicken Dinner"

After school, Renie went to the market place, to Auntie Fanny. She was welcomed with hugs and kissed by both Mama and Auntie Fanny, who even gave her a present, a new student cap. Renie loved it.

Mama also had some good news for Renie. Mrs. and Mr. Landau had invited Renie and Mama for Shabbat dinner, with chicken soup and kneidlach. "Like the ones Nana made?" Renie asked.

"We will see," Mama answered.

She asked Auntie Fanny what time Shabbat began, and they walked home looking forward to their Shabbat dinner.

Friday evening at six o'clock, they were both ready, dressed in their best clothes, with the flowers that Mamma had bought from Auntie Fanny. They set off.

Renie did not remember when she had last been so happy. She felt like she could fly in the air. She was so looking forward to a dinner with other people—she could almost taste the chicken soup with kneidlach, hoping they would taste like Nana's.

She could not wait to get to the Landaus' house.

When they reached the Landau family's beautiful house, Mama knocked on the door.

It was opened by Mrs. Landau. She stood in the doorway and said, "My dear, I am so sorry, we just finished eating. We ate early today. There is nothing left but chicken bones, but you are welcome to some chicken soup with kneidlach."

Mama just stood by the door. Renie so wanted chicken soup with kneidlach. Then she heard Mama say, "That is alright, we have dinner at home, don't worry." She gave the flowers to Mrs. Landau and said, "These are for you, for Shabbat."

Mama took Renie by the hand. The door shut behind them, and they started their walk home.

"I will never set foot in this house again," Renie heard Mama say.

Reine cried all the way home. Mama did not go to the Landau family's house to cook for them ever again.

She had lost her job.

Chapter 27
The Storm

The weather was getting cooler; it was windy and sometimes it rained. The walk to school seemed a little longer, and it was less pleasant. Mama noticed that Renie's sweater was not enough to keep her warm. She told Renie that next week, when they got their "package," there might be a coat for her to keep her warm. "Will it be a red coat?" she asked.

"Maybe," Mama said.

Renie imagined herself in a new red coat and somehow felt a little more comfortable for the rest of the walk to school. Her coat would be the "best" one in the class.

The last week of September drew to an end. The next day was cloudy and the weather kept getting colder.

After school, Renie walked with Mama to the post office to get their monthly package. When Mama picked it up, she said, "It is lighter than usual. It must be clothes, maybe even a red coat for you?"

Had Renie's dream come true, she wondered?

They swiftly walked home.

When they reached home, they quickly put the package on the kitchen table and opened it.

The package was full of ties. Nothing but ties!

Mama turned over the package, to see if there was anything else at the bottom, but there were only ties, nothing but ties.

Mama collapsed on the kitchen chair and began to cry. "Who on earth buys ties?" she sobbed. "What will we eat this whole month? How will we survive?"

She left all the ties on the kitchen table, some of which fell to the floor, and ran sobbing to the bedroom.

Renie heard her crying until it got dark, but she did not dare knock on the door.

Renie switched on the kitchen light, put the kettle on, made tea, and prepared supper.

It wasn't until much later that she dared knock on the bedroom door. There was no answer. Slowly, very quietly, she opened the door. "Mama, I prepared supper for us," she whispered.

"You eat. I cannot eat, I want to sleep," was the answer.

Renie left the bedroom. She went back to the kitchen, put all the ties back inside the package, and sat down to eat her supper alone.

Renie woke up the next morning. The sun's rays were shining through the window. It was Sunday. Renie, for once, was glad there was no school. She would stay home with Mama.

Renie spent the whole day at home. She played with her dolls, did some homework and tried to cheer Mama up, but she did not react. She only wanted to sleep and to be left alone.

Then Renie had an idea. She woke Mama and said there was no lunch, what should she do? Mama answered that there was bread, cheese, and milk, and that she should eat that.

"But Mama, I already had bread, cheese, and milk for supper and for breakfast. It's all gone."

"Can't you understand that I am tired? All I want to do is sleep. I cannot fight anymore. I give up, leave me alone!"

Renie cried and left the room. She had never heard Mama talk like that. She had no one to turn to. She was all alone and she was afraid.

Mama kept sleeping all through the day and night.

Renie ate whatever was left in the house and went to bed. She listened to Mama's breathing and fell asleep.

She was hoping for a new day—maybe then things would change.

On Monday, Renie woke up to find Mama out of bed. She immediately jumped up and found her mother in the bathroom taking a bath. Renie was so relieved. Then she turned around and found a meal on the table, all set, just ready to eat.

Renie got ready for school and waited for Mama to come to the table. When she came out of the bathroom, she said to Renie, "I cannot take you to school today. You will have to stay home. Maybe tomorrow. Eat your breakfast."

"I will not eat if you don't eat with me," Renie said.

"Do as you like," Mama said, and returned to the bedroom.

Renie was hungry but she didn't eat. When Mama woke, much later, she went to the bathroom. That's when Mama noticed the kitchen table—it was just as she had left it that morning.

She found Renie playing with her two dolls. One was an old rag doll, with two buttons for eyes, and the other was a carved wooden doll. Renie was talking to the rag doll, saying, "Look at you, you are old and ugly. You don't even have eyes, and your clothes are dirty. I don't want you anymore. I will not play with you."

Mama just stood there, her cheeks wet with tears. Renie turned around and asked. "Why are you crying again?"

"I feel like this rag doll. I am no good to you anymore. I cannot even be a mother."

Renie jumped up from the floor, hugged Mama, and cried with her.

"I promise I will never throw my old rag doll away. I will always love her."

Chapter 28
Friendship

That day Mama did not cry. She talked with Reine, explaining that she was worried that they had very little money, not even enough to buy food. She said, "I did not want to worry you, but how will we live till the end of the month?"

"I know," Renie said, "I will try to sell some ties. Auntie Fanny will help and we will have money to buy food."

Mama's eyes filled with tears. She hugged Renie close to her chest and cried again, but it was different this time. She did not sob. Instead, she said quietly, "What would I do without you?" And she kissed Renie again and again.

The next morning, Renie awoke to the smell of food—fried eggs! She jumped out of bed and quickly went to the kitchen.

Mama was dressed, preparing breakfast, and she smiled. "Good morning," she said, and when she saw Renie's look of surprise, she explained, "I went to the little store down the street to buy bread and milk." 'Anything else?' the saleslady asked, and when I explained that I had no money, she said, 'My dear, take everything you need, and you can pay me when you have money.' Isn't she a beautiful person? Today, we eat."

They sat down to a wonderful breakfast, smiling, talking, laughing.

Renie was so happy to go to school. Her friends and teachers greeted her and asked how she was.

Renie felt wanted; she felt important.

When she finished her school day, she went to Auntie Fanny who greeted her with a big hug and kisses. She asked how she was, how Mama was, why she hadn't seen them for a few days. Renie began to tell Auntie Fanny what had happened, that Mama had cried for days and wouldn't get out of bed, that they didn't have enough money to buy food, that the lady in the store, who was a beautiful person, let Mama take everything she needed and said she could pay next month, that today they had eaten a wonderful breakfast and she had gone to school.

"But where is Mama now? Why isn't she here to take me home?" Renie asked.

"I will take you home," Auntie Fanny said. After some time, Auntie Fanny took Renie home.

When they reached the house, they found the door locked. Auntie Fanny knocked on the door again and again, calling Mama's name. Renie also called for Mama, at the top of her voice. Then Auntie Fanny kicked the door and Mama opened it.

She had been asleep the whole day.

Auntie Fanny walked in, with a basket full of fruit, vegetables, and eggs. She put it on the kitchen table and turned to Mama and said in a loud voice, "What do you think you are doing? We have known each other our whole lives and you couldn't tell me about your problem?"

As soon as Auntie Fanny starting to shout, Renie ran to the bedroom. She didn't want to hear Auntie Fanny shout at Mama, but she couldn't help hearing, even though the door was shut.

"You have lost your entire family, do you want to lose that child too?"

Renie could hear Mama crying. She wanted to go to her, to tell Auntie Fanny that she would take care of her, but she didn't open the bedroom door.

After a while the shouting stopped and Renie carefully opened the door. She saw Auntie Fanny and Mama in each other's arms. They were both crying.

Renie left the bedroom and walked towards them. She hugged them both for a long time. When they all let go and relaxed, Auntie Fanny smiled and said, "And now let's make supper and eat!"

It was the best supper Renie could remember.

Chapter 29
A Sense of Smell

The next morning, Renie woke up very early. She had to prepare her little suitcase to fill it with ties, so Mama could bring it to Auntie Fanny, and Renie could sell ties after school.

After breakfast, they both set off to school. Renie was excited but a little worried. How would she sell the ties? Would she shout to the passersby like she heard others do? If so, what would she say?

Then it came to her. She made up a jingle, which went like this:

Krawaty, krawaty!

Za pieniadze I na raty.

Komu. Komu.

Bo ide do domu.

Which meant:

Ties, ties!

For cash or credit.

Who wants to buy

To get home must I.

Renie did not remember much of school that day! She had too many "butterflies" in her stomach. When school was over she quickly went to Auntie Fanny's stall where Mama was waiting for her with the suitcase.

Renie made a little show for Mama and Auntie Fanny. They both laughed at the jingle and said it was funny.

Renie went to work. She put the suitcase on a chair, which Auntie Fanny brought her. She opened it, put a few ties over the lid of the suitcase, and stood in front of Auntie Fanny's stall.

Many people were walking past the little girl and smiled at her, but no one really paid much attention to the ties.

She decided to use her jingle. Now people stopped, listened to her, looked at the ties, and smiled, but no one wanted to buy them. It was getting dark. Renie had to go home. She put all the ties in the suitcase and gave it to Auntie Fanny to keep for her.

"You are such a brave little girl. Don't worry, tomorrow is another day. Maybe the sun will shine for you tomorrow. Remember that you always have your job if you want it," Auntie Fanny said. She gave Renie a big hug and an apple and kissed her on her cheek.

Mama took Renie home. On the way she bought her a big ice cream cone. It was delicious.

The next day was a little better. One nice man stopped and asked her how much a tie cost. When she told him, he asked if she would sell it for less. She told him that it was a pure silk tie, so she could not sell it for less, and the nice man said sorry and walked away. When Renie told Auntie Fanny about it, she said, "Don't you worry, he'll be back."

The next day, the man came back and bought the tie.

Renie was beside herself. She had done it! She'd won! She had sold a tie!

Days passed. The weather was getting colder.

One day, when Renie finished school it was cold. She walked quickly to keep warm. When she reached Auntie Fanny's stall, Auntie Fanny gave her a hug and kissed her on the head. Auntie Fanny said, "There is something for you in the back. Have a look."

Renie wondered what could be in the back for her. She went to the back, and there was a large carton. She opened it and heard a long, loud scream. She did not realize she was the one who was screaming.

In the carton was the most beautiful red coat she had ever seen. She put it on. It was cozy, the warmest coat in the world. It also had such a pleasant smell! She walked over to Auntie Fanny, who had the biggest smile on her face. She hugged Renie for a long time. "Wear it in good health, my dear. I love you so."

Renie wore her coat with pride.

After school Renie kept selling ties. Sometimes she sold a few, sometime none.

Then, one day, as she was laying out the ties, choosing the ones she liked, she noticed a pair of tall black boots. Renie froze. She had seen them before, on a Nazi officer, but the war was over, so it couldn't be! Slowly she lifted her eyes she saw a pair of brown breeches covered by a black leather coat. This was no Nazi officer! She raised her eyes higher and saw the bluest eyes she had ever seen. He looked at the ties, then at her, and asked, "How much for a tie?"

"Ten zloty," she said.

"I will give you a hundred if you choose one for me and put it on," he said.

For once Renie did not know what to say—she would have to ask Mama. "Wait here, please. Take care of my ties."

She ran as fast as her legs would carry her. When she got to Mama, she asked Mama what she should do. "He must be a nice man. He sees a nice little girl and wants to help. It's all right," Mama said.

Renie ran back and there was the nice man waiting for her. She searched for a tie that would go with his eyes, which were so blue. When she found one that she liked, she put the suitcase aside and climbed onto the chair. He bent over to help her put the tie around his neck. She had to stand on her toes, and as she came closer, something hit her—a familiar smell!

She moved still closer and sniffed his neck, to get more of the smell.

He pulled back. "What are you doing, child?"

"You smell like my Papa, but he is dead the Germans killed him," she answered.

"How old are you, child?" he asked.

"I'll be six soon," she answered.

"What's your name?" he asked.

"Renie," she said.

"Where's your mother?"

"Mama is in the back with Auntie Fanny."

"What's your mama's name?"

"Ella," she answered.

"Can you take me to her?"

"What about the tie?" she asked.

"Here is the money. I'll put on your tie."

He picked Renie up and asked her to lead him to Mama. When they reached Auntie Fanny's stall, Mama turned around and cried out, "Alex!" and she fainted.

"Papa came for me, just like he promised," Renie softly whispered to herself.

Epilogue
The Leather Coat

They separated when she was two,
Her and her dad,
Though she could not let go of him,
The love for him she had.
He gave her his coat of leather,
His smell entwined.
With that she was comforted,
With that and a box she could successfully hide.
For three years she hid,
And she was almost found;
But she hid under the leather coat
And did not make a sound.
At five her mother took her,
Father and his job were gone.
So they opened up a tie stand;

They knew that they had won.

One day a man came in,

He asked questions about their lives.

But the little girl was stubborn

And first made him try on some ties.

While she fitted his ties,

There was a smell she knew;

It was of the leather coat,

That smell she loved and with it grew.

Her heart beat fast,

It wouldn't skip a beat.

"You are my father," she said.

At last they finally meet.

Poem written by Mai Dror, Renie's granddaughter.